The American Frontier

Images and Myths

Patricia Hills

Whitney Museum of American Art

June 26 to September 16, 1973

Cover detail. George Caleb Bingham. *Daniel Boone
Escorting Settlers Through the Cumberland Gap,*
1851-52. Oil on canvas, 36 x 52. Washington University
Gallery of Art, St. Louis

Acknowledgments

Many have assisted me in my researches. For their continuing enthusiasm and support I want especially to thank Roxana Barry Alger, Larry Curry, Carl S. Dentzel, Frank G. Hathaway, George Neubert, and William S. Truettner. Others who have been most helpful in securing loans and in bringing to my attention new material are Barbara Susan Chandler, Wanda Corn, Marilyn Drucker, Edward H. Dwight, Sarah Faunce, Stuart P. Feld, Frederick D. Hill, Donelson F. Hoopes, Catherine Hoover, Cecily Langdale, Laura Luckey, James H. Maroney, Maria Naylor, Dorothy Phillips, Guy St. Clair, Lewis A. Shepherd, Natalie Spassky, Roger B. Stein, Frank Trapp, Robert Vose Jr., Ila Weiss, and Professor Stephen Williams. I want also to thank John I. H. Baur, Helen Ferrulli and Frederic Hills who read the essay and made many constructive suggestions. Finally, my gratitude to Sue Feld, Patricia Hamilton, and especially Mariann Nowack for their help during the planning of the exhibition and the preparation of the catalogue.

The essay is dedicated to the memory of Robert Goldwater.

Patricia Hills

Frontispiece. Emanuel Leutze. *Westward the Course of Empire Takes Its Way*, 1861. Oil on canvas, 33 3/8 x 44 3/8. National Collection of Fine Arts, Smithsonian Institution, Washington, D. C., Bequest of Miss Sara Carr Upton

The American Frontier: Images and Myths

Beginning with the westward migration of Anglo-Europeans across the Atlantic, America took on the dimensions of myth. Confronting the early settlers was not just the reality of a different geography and climate, but the promise of a "*new* world"—where man could shed the corrupting influences of an over-refined society, forget his previous mistakes, and be reborn into innocence. Both the reality and the myth of America as a frontier—as a new, only partially civilized, land would become a major theme in American painting in the second and third quarters of the nineteenth century. And since the frontier experience has been considered as one of the shaping forces in the development of the American character, the frontier theme in art merits examination against its own cultural background of literary antecedents, mid-century political pronouncements, historical events and the artists' own individual predispositions.

The idealist philosopher Bishop George Berkeley, early in the eighteenth century, proposed a scheme for establishing an experimental college in Bermuda to convert the American Indians, subjects he considered more worthy of "enlightenment" than the citizens of his native Ireland. Berkeley's poem "Verses on the Prospect of Planting Arts and Learning in America," written about 1726, expressed the yearnings of many eighteenth-century intellectuals for a new Golden Age. To Berkeley, the new world represented the "seat of innocence/ Where nature guides and virtue rules . . . not such as Europe breeds in her decay." The sixth and final stanza of the poem proclaims America as the grand culmination of the progress of civilization:

> Westward the course of empire takes its way;
> The four first Acts already past,
> A fifth shall close the Drama with the day;
> Time's noblest offspring is the last.[1]

"Westward the course of empire" became the resounding chorus throughout the nineteenth century; in the 1860s Emanuel Leutze paid homage to Berkeley's sentiments when he painted his own apotheosis of the theme for the Capitol in Washington, D. C. (frontispiece).

In the hundred years following Berkeley's unrealized educational plans, the colonists along the Atlantic Coast increased in number, cultivated farms, established businesses and a maritime commerce and threw off the economic and political domination of Europe. Supported by the patronage of a newly prosperous middle class, the arts flowered. Poets and painters rallied to the cause of a national school of the arts which would be as independent of Europe as was commerce and industry. Ralph Waldo Emerson in his essay "The Poet" of 1842 called on artists to turn their attention to regional subjects: "America is a poem in our eyes, its ample geography dazzles the imagination."[2]

Responding to the plea for a national art, the landscape artist Thomas Cole[3] proclaimed in his "Essay on American Scenery" of 1835 that "the most distinctive, and perhaps the most impressive, characteristic of American scenery is its wildness."[4] Indeed, upon the eve of his departure for Europe in 1829, Cole was cautioned by his friend the poet William Cullen Bryant to "keep that earlier, wilder image bright."[5] To these poets and artists of the early nineteenth century, the wilderness—wild, rugged, untouched by picturesque and cultivated touches—was irrefutably *the* American landscape.

Cole emphasized this wildness in his *American Lake Scene* (fig. 1) of 1844 in which the small accessory figure of an Indian locates the scene in the New World. Asher B. Durand in his "Letters to Young Painters" of 1855 reiterated the superior qualities of raw American nature:

> Go not abroad then in search of material for the exercise of your pencil, while the virgin charms of our native land have claims on your deepest affections. Many are the flowers in our untrodden wilds that have blushed too long unseen.... The "lone and tranquil" lakes embosomed in ancient forests, that abound in our wild districts, the unshorn mountains surrounding them with their richly-textured covering, the ocean prairies of the West, and the many other forms of Nature yet spared from the pollutions of civilization, afford a guarantee for a reputation of originality that you may elsewhere long seek and find not.[6]

His comments, published in the prestigious art magazine *The Crayon*, influenced a generation of painters to look to their home surroundings for scenes and themes. Durand's painting *The American Wilderness* (fig. 2) of 1864 captures both the reality and the mood of a quiet wilderness unravaged by civilized man.

Joshua Shaw had earlier represented the arcadian aspect of the wilderness and its native inhabitants, the Indians, in his *On the Susquehanna* (fig. 3) of 1839. The intimidating approach of the white man's culture, however, disturbs the pastoral tranquility in Shaw's *Coming of the White Man*, in which Indians recoil at the sight of the ship, a ghostly apparition moving up the waterway. With its gently graded luminist tones and its quietly moving Indians, peacefulness pervades Sanford Gifford's *In the Wilderness* (fig. 4) of 1860. As the eastern seaboard became more populated and cultivated, artists seeking virgin forests and wild life retreated to the mountains of the Catskills and the Adirondacks. Indians completely disappeared in James Hart's vision of untouched nature, *The Adirondacks*, to be replaced by gamboling bears.

Many artists were attracted to the region where the Indian lived and hunted, beyond the area of colonial settlement. The first known European to record the western shore of the new continent was John Webber, a Swiss artist who sailed on the third voyage of Captain James Cook. Webber's *Nootka Sound* of 1784 was reconstructed from sketches made of the scenery and Indians when Cook's ship anchored along the the Northwest Coast in 1778.

Other early nineteenth-century artists joined scouting and surveying expeditions to sketch the uncharted territories of the western United States and Canada. Joining the expedition of Major Stephen H. Long in 1819, Titian Ramsay Peale made studies of Indian villages and animals (fig. 5). Samuel Seymour journeyed with Major Long's party in 1819-20 up the South Platte, and again in 1823 to northern Minnesota and Manitoba, sketching the topography and, as in *Pawnee Council*, scenes of the Major's own exchanges with the Indians.

Government pronouncements as early as 1824 predicting the rapid extinction of Indians[7] and stories in the popular magazines lamenting the fate of "the last Indian"[8] prompted artists to record on canvas and paper the specific characteristics and color of the various Indian tribes. The German artist Carl Bodmer[9] traveled west with the adventurer and naturalist Maximilian, Prince of Wied, in 1833-34, and his watercolors were published in 1839 as aquatints to illustrate Maximilian's *Journey into the Interior of North America*. Alfred J. Miller accompanied Captain William Drummond Stewart in 1837 and produced hundreds of watercolors and drawings. To Miller, and indeed to the majority of artists, the sketches done in the West became source material for later, more elaborate and romantic studio paintings. In Miller's

Beating a Retreat (fig. 9), for example, the colorful but wounded warrior and his frightened, galloping hobby-horse merge into one fanciful image of futile flight set against the pink and blue backdrop of a summer day.

George Catlin, who journeyed on several expeditions up the Missouri River into the northwestern interior beginning in 1832, executed the most impressive paintings of Indian life. Catlin's portraits of proud tribal chiefs and their wives are among the most important visual and ethnographic records of the last century, and his writings, beginning with his fully illustrated, two-volume *Manners, Customs, and Condition of the North American Indians* of 1841, stimulated concern about the true plight of Indians. (With the passage of the Indian Removal Bill in 1830 the Indians were already being pushed westward by a series of enforced land exchanges.)[10] Catlin's encyclopedic attempt to render all aspects of Indian life on the prairies resulted in a series of reconstructions of events both witnessed and imagined, both factual and lyrical. It is improbable that Catlin had viewed such a scene as *Sioux Indians on Snowshoes Lancing Buffalo* (fig. 7), yet his vision of the event, with the dark, diminishing shapes of fleeing buffalo on a cold, bleak, snowy terrain, epitomizes the hardships of winter subsistence for the Sioux. In *Buffalo Chase—Bull Protecting Cow and Calf* (fig. 8) the contorted silhouettes of the horses express the agony of the buffalo hunt. In *Prairie Bluffs Burning* (fig. 6), with its red burning grass, its charred, black fields, its smoking hills, and its frightened, leaping animals, Catlin synthesizes the process of and the flight from conflagration.

Other artists who studied and painted Indian life included Seth Eastman, an Army officer stationed at western posts in the 1830s and 1840s, and John Mix Stanley, who roamed both the southwest and the northwestern territories as an itinerant painter in the 1840s and 1850s. Eastman's *Lacrosse Playing Among the Sioux Indians* (fig. 11) with its fidelity of detail contrasts with his *Indian on the Lookout*, with its dramatic implications of impending danger. Similarly, Stanley's modest sketches of Indian life, *Assiniboin Encampment on the Upper Missouri* and *A Halt on the Prairie for a Smoke* (fig. 10), contrast with the tense moment of attack—the drama of death—in his *A Buffalo Hunt on the Southwestern Prairie* (fig. 24). Few, indeed, were those early painters who did not exploit the melodramatic possibilities of Indian life. Henry F. Farny repainted his 1881 composition *The Last Vigil* (fig. 12) as a *Harper's Weekly* illustration of 1891, entitled *The Last Scene of the Last Act of the Sioux War: The Pine Ridge Massacre of 1890.*[11]

But the concept of "the frontier" embraced more than the unexplored wilderness and more than Indian camps and hunting grounds. The historian Frederick Jackson Turner, whose address "The Significance of the Frontier in American History" in 1892 brought about a reevaluation of the "meaning" of the West, defined the frontier as "the meeting point between savagery and civilization."[12] Turner further distinguished between the frontiers of the traders, farmers, miners, and ranchers, and postulated that each frontier had contained simultaneously a wild and a cultivated aspect. A perusal of the art of the frontier reveals that his categories apply as well to mid-century paintings.

After the Lewis and Clark expedition of 1804-06 into northwest territory, the literary imagination of writers focused on the trapper (often called "the mountain man") as an appropriate symbol of the advancing frontier. The Leather-stocking novels of James Fenimore Cooper stirred Thomas Cole to paint several scenes from Cooper's *The Last of the Mohicans* (fig. 13). To the early nineteenth-century romantic artists Charles Deas, Arthur F. Tait, and Alvan Fisher the trapper's life was characterized by imminent danger. Rapids and tangled underbrush present obstacles for the trapper in Deas' *The Voyageurs* (fig. 14), and premonitions of unseen dangers alert the scout in Arthur F. Tait's *American Frontier Life* (fig. 16).

But the most explicit threat was the omnipresent Indian suggested in Alvan Fisher's *Trappers Discover the Smoke of an Indian Camp* (fig. 15).

The most famous scout, and most represented in art, was Daniel Boone (1734-1820), who grew to the stature of folk hero in the early nineteenth century as a result of several adulatory biographies and fictional representations. His reputation for courage and determination had its basis in fact; in terms of myth, he represented the frontiersman who had fled the confines of settled society to lead the citizens of America to a new, more democratic civilization.[13] In William Ranney's *Daniel Boone's First View of Kentucky* (fig. 17) of 1849 the old scout points out the view of Kentucky from the Cumberland Gap. Ranney's *Squire Boone Crossing the Mountains with Stores for His Brother Daniel, Encamped in the Wilds of Kentucky* (fig. 18) of 1852 illustrates a later episode of Boone's life in the spring of 1770.[14]

In George Caleb Bingham's *Daniel Boone Escorting Settlers Through the Cumberland Gap* (fig. 19) of 1851-52, a latter-day Moses leads his people forward through a hostile environment to the promised land.[15] The Cumberland Gap, a fissure in the mountains of eastern Tennessee near the Kentucky border, was a famous passage for travelers, but its reputation as one of the gateways to progress had extraordinary staying power. Turner might have visualized Bingham's painting when he rhapsodized:

> Stand at the Cumberland Gap and watch the procession of civilization, marching single file—the buffalo following the trail to the salt springs, the Indian, the fur-trader and hunter, the cattle-raiser, the pioneer farmer—and the frontier has passed by.[16]

To Americans moving west to clear and settle and acquire land, the scout was a necessity. Heroes in myth, in reality scouts gained the reputation of being shiftless vagrants, outside the law, too irresponsible to own and cultivate their own land.[17] They sprang from the same milieu as "squatters," the early pioneers who had settled on the public domain. George Caleb Bingham, a Whig opposed to the extension of the suffrage to the propertyless classes,[18] painted *The Squatters* (fig. 20) in 1850, writing as follows regarding them:

> The Squatters as a class, are not fond of the toil of agriculture, but erect their rude Cabins upon those remote portions of the National domain, where abundant game supplies their phisical [sic] wants. When this source of subsistance becomes diminished, in consequence of increasing settlements around, they usually sell out their slight improvement, with their 'preemption title' to the land, and again follow the receding footsteps of [the] Savage.[19]

Bingham and others condescended to the squatters, comparing them with Indians, because the squatters did not sufficiently value property or cultivate the soil.[20]

The cultivators of the soil, the farmers, became the subject matter for a number of New York-based artists. Thomas Cole had said:

> ...The cultivated [scenery] must not be forgotten, for it is still more important to man in his social capacity—necessarily bringing him in contact with the cultured; it encompasses our homes, and, though devoid of the stern sublimity of the wild, its quieter spirit steals tenderly into our bosoms mingled with a thousand domestic affections and heart-touching associations....[21]

Since the overriding myth in America was the necessity of the progress of civilization,[22] it is not surprising that the farmer, the cultivator, became the truly heroic figure in the imagination of mid-nineteenth-century America. The rustic returning to his log cabin in Thomas Cole's *Home in the Woods* (fig. 21), was the American Adam celebrated in the poems of Walt Whitman's *Leaves of Grass* of 1855. Cole's pupil Frederic Church painted a similar log cabin, nestled securely in a grove of trees, in *Scene in the Catskill Mountains* (fig. 22) before turning his attention to the more exotic topography of South America. And Sanford Gifford's *Twilight on Hunter Mountain* (fig. 23) expressed the quiet sanctitude of the rural endeavor.

As important as the New England farm may have been for maintaining the mythic correlation of agricultural work and national virtue, many artists looked westward past the Mississippi River to the excitement of life on the moving frontier—to the "meeting point between savagery and civilization." Visual metaphors became established: Indians represented savagery and excitement; pioneers (and later Union troops) represented civilization and destiny.

Excitement on the plains was represented in the buffalo hunts of John Mix Stanley (fig. 24) and Charles Wimar (fig. 25). William Ranney, who saw Army service in Texas, returned to the East in 1837 and drew upon his western experiences for his art. His paintings only occasionally included Indians, but his *Hunting Wild Horses* (fig. 26) of 1846 expresses the romantic excitement of the West.

A recurring and popular theme was the threatening presence of Indians. George Caleb Bingham's *The Concealed Enemy* of 1845, Johannes Adam Simon Oertel's *The War Path* (fig. 28) of 1855, and Jules Tavernier's more ambitious *Attack by Indians near Chimney Rock* (fig. 30) all represent the stealth which was the Indians' reputation. The actual moment of attack was most dramatically portrayed in Charles Wimar's *The Attack on an Emigrant Train* (fig. 29), painted in Düsseldorf in 1856.

Other dangers lurked unexpectedly on the prairies. Charles Deas' *The Prairie Fire* (fig. 27) of 1847 became the occasion for the depiction of male gallantry; A. J. Miller's *The Lost Greenhorn* represented the hazards of over-confidence. Ranney's sentimental *Prairie Burial* with its small, child's grave became a reminder of the sorrows of emigration. And George Brewerton's surreal *Mojave Desert* (fig. 31) with its scorched, yellow terrain—the visualization of "The Great American Desert"—conjured up images of exhaustion and death.

By mid-century the country was caught up in the spirit of westward expansion. Thomas Hart Benton, Senator from Missouri from 1821 to 1851, had argued for the necessity of establishing overland trade routes to the Pacific. His son-in-law John Charles Frémont headed an expedition to the Rocky Mountains in 1842 with Kit Carson as a guide and later explored Oregon, Nevada and California. Migration increased along the Oregon Trail in the mid-1840s and with the territories of Oregon and California secured in 1846 and 1848, the United States had reached the natural boundary of the Pacific. William Gilpin, friend of Benton, companion of Frémont and first territorial governor of Colorado, was the most flamboyant advocate of western expansion. Believing that geography determined social progress, he wrote in 1846:

> The *untransacted* destiny of the American people is to subdue the continent—to rush over this vast field to the Pacific Ocean—to animate the many hundred millions of its people, and to cheer them upward . . . —to agitate these herculean masses—to establish a new order in human affairs . . . —to regenerate superannuated nations— . . . to stir up the sleep of a hundred centuries—to teach old nations a new civilization—to confirm the destiny of the human race—to carry the career of

mankind to its culminating point—to cause a stagnant people to be reborn—to perfect science—to emblazon history with the conquest of peace—to shed a new and resplendent glory upon mankind—to unite the world in one social family—to dissolve the spell of tyranny and exalt charity—to absolve the curse that weighs down humanity, and to shed blessings round the world![23]

Of course expansion had to be followed by the hard work of developing the land. Subsequent to Gilpin's agitations, the Homestead Act was passed by Congress in 1862, granting a settler 160 acres of public land after five years of residence and the payment of nominal fees.[24]

In art, the spirit of "manifest destiny" is best exemplified in the mural by Emanuel Leutze for the Capitol entitled *Westward the Course of Empire Takes Its Way*. The small sketch (frontispiece) for the mural represents pioneer men, women and children about to cross a pass high in the mountains from which they sight green fertile valleys below. The sun-bleached bones strewn along the path and the burial scene at the right refer to the victims of emigration, but the infant cradled by its mother at left center stirs hope for the future. The small scene below is of Golden Gate Bay, which is the port of San Francisco and the gateway to the Orient.

There were other paintings of heroic pioneers undisturbed by either Indian attack or devastation from the elements. William Ranney's *Advice on the Prairie* (fig. 35)[25] of 1853 and Benjamin Franklin Rinehart's *The Emigrant Train Bedding Down for the Night* (fig. 36) of 1867 represent the pioneers at work even in the pause from their journeys. Samuel Colman's prodigious *Ships of the Plains* (fig. 37) of 1872, with its straining teams of oxen, illustrates most graphically the pioneer spirit of determination and endurance, even though by that time the days of the great migrations of wagon trains had passed.

In the late 1860s the "winning of the West" meant the completion of the transcontinental railway, an event followed with the same interest in the eastern press as the moon shots have been in the late 1960s. Between 1848 and 1853 Thomas Hart Benton had urged Congress to construct the Pacific Railroad "as a national work, on a scale commensurate with its grandeur."[26] But Stephen Douglas fought on the side of private enterprise and persuaded the government to turn over large parcels of land to eastern entrepreneurs.[27] After the Civil War, railway construction accelerated, and the Central Pacific and the Union Pacific met at Promontory Point, Utah, on May 10, 1869, for the ceremonial completion. Thomas Rossiter's *Opening of the Wilderness* (fig. 32), with its railroad trains waiting at dusk, signals popular sentiment regarding the importance of the train for the implementation of "manifest destiny."[28] Thomas Otter's *On the Road* (fig. 33) of 1860 graphically depicts the advantages of the railroad over the covered wagon jostling inefficiently over dirt roads. However, the train was as susceptible to sabotage as the covered wagon; in Theodor Kaufmann's *Railway Train Attacked by Indians* (fig. 34), avenging Indians derail an approaching train. Ultimately the establishment of a network of railroads and the deployment of Union troops to protect that network meant the end of the open range for the Indian.

In the decades following the Civil War many of the major landscape painters—Albert Bierstadt, Sanford Gifford, Worthington Whittredge, Samuel Colman and Thomas Moran—went west with expeditions, painting scenes of the campsites on the plains and along the rivers. Bierstadt's *Platte River, Nebraska* (fig. 38), Colman's *Emigrant Train, Colorado* (fig. 40) and Whittredge's *On the Plains, Colorado* (fig. 41) appear to be accurate transcriptions of the broad expanse of plains approaching the range of the Rocky Mountains. Whittredge, however, was more than willing to tamper with the natural topography of the land for the exigencies of his art. Writing about his *Crossing the Ford, Platte River, Colorado* (fig. 39) (engraved in 1871 as *The Rocky Mountains* for William Cullen Bryant's *Picturesque America*), Whittredge recalled the progress of the painting:

> ...I went twice to the Rocky Mountains after my first visit, these last times by railroad. The first of these visits was undertaken because I had gotten into some trouble with one of my pictures. On my first visit to Denver I had made a sketch from near our camping ground, from which I had begun a large picture. I had introduced the Platte River in the foreground and looking out from under a group of trees were seen the plains and in the distance the snow-capped mountains; some Indian tents and a party of Indians crossing the stream completing the composition. The trees did not suit me. I remembered a group I had seen on the Cache la Poudre River, fifty miles from Denver, which I thought would suit my picture better. I undertook the journey to make sketches of them. They were finally introduced into the picture, much to its improvement.[29]

Thomas Moran's views of the West were also adjusted to heighten the color and drama of the natural topography.[30] The art critic S. W. G. Benjamin, describing Moran's *The Mirage* of 1879 (fig. 42) as "a sublime, isolated peak, cloven in the center, that soars like a Titanic Feudal tower above the banks of the Green River,"[31] found other words of praise for Moran's art:

> While he reverences the local truth of a scene, conscious that it is impossible for man to improve the creations of the Almighty, he so renders it as to give it the unmistakable stamp of his own mind and style, and invests it with the poetic sentiment of a highly-wrought imagination.[32]

When gold was discovered in California in 1848, the population numbered less than 18,000.[33] The rush to "Eldorado" began, attracting adventurers, speculators and a number of artists. Infected by the national fever, William Sidney Mount, who rarely ventured further west than the Hudson River, painted *California News* (fig. 43) in 1850. To artists in California, the mining camp was more lucrative as a pictorial source than as one of direct remuneration. Getting to the sites, however, was often a strenuous ordeal, as depicted in Eugen Camere's amusing genre scene *Mike Shuler's Freighting Outfit*. To many, prospectors were heroic characters—men with vision and unafraid of action as depicted in Martin's *The Forty-Niners* (fig. 45) with the two figures poised on the summit of the mountain. Joseph Harrington's *Discovery of the Comstock Lode* (fig. 44) of 1875 celebrates an historic event: Henry T. P. Comstock and his companions are shown as they may have been in 1859 when they established their claim to the rich, Nevada silver deposit.

The majority of genre scenes of miners depict the men during moments of relaxation, as in A. D. O. Browere's *South of Tuolomme City* (fig. 48), or of camaraderie, as in Ernest Narjot's *Gold Rush Camp* (fig. 47) of 1882 and Cassilly Adams' *Playing Cards*. Rufus Wright's *The Card Players* (fig. 46) of 1882, however, represents ruthless skulduggery in which the loser threatens the incredulous winner. Such men were satirized in Mark Twain's *Roughing It* of 1871 and in Bret Harte's humorous "The Luck of Roaring

Camp" and other gold rush stories he wrote in the 1870s. Thus, the inspiration for the genre paintings of the 1880s was probably more literary than actually observed.[34]

What most distinguished California after the ride over the deserts of Nevada was the spectacular scenery—particularly Yosemite Valley, the High Sierra Mountains, and the giant sequoia trees. Bierstadt traveled to the Pacific state in 1863 and again in 1871, making oil studies of the mountains and valleys which were later developed into scenes of grandiosity and, at times, banality. But a regional landscape school also flourished, led by Thomas Hill and William Keith whose prolific productions of views helped popularize the state as a tourist attraction. Hill's *Yosemite Valley* (fig. 51), Keith's *California Pines* (fig. 50) and Edwin Deakin's *Mount Tallac* (fig. 49) suggest California as a land both of adventure and of peaceful retreat.

William Hahn chose the High Sierras as the setting for the genre scenes *Return from the Hunt, Sierras* (fig. 52) and *Return from the Bear Hunt* (fig. 53). Edward Vischer's *Giant Sequoia*, with its dislocations of scale, projects the awesome largeness of the thousand-year-old trees.

The Hispanic past of "Old California" and the rancher's frontier converged in the paintings of James Walker. The cowhands dressed in Mexican costumes in his *Vaqueros at the Roundup* (fig. 56) and his *Californios at the Horse Roundup* (fig. 57) were the precursors for the cowboys of Frederic Remington and Charles Russell. Otto Sommer's 1867-68 painting *Westward Ho!* (fig. 54), depicting tired but valiant cowhands leading short-horned cattle through the dusty plains to the West to improve the stock, contrasts with William Hahn's *Mexican Cattle Drivers* (fig. 55), of 1883 in which Mexican ranch hands jauntily ride down the mountain with their well-fed steers.

The city of the West in the nineteenth century was San Francisco. William Hahn's *Market Scene, Sansome Street, San Francisco* (fig. 58)[35] is a pictorial synthesis of the frontier city's sprawling market with its display of varied and abundant agricultural products, its diverse nationalities and classes, and its hint of emerging cultural styles. The painting finds its verbal equivalent in Walt Whitman's "Song of the Redwood-Tree" of 1874:

> The flashing and golden pageant of California,
> The sudden and gorgeous drama, the sunny and ample lands,
> The long and varied stretch from Puget Sound to Colorado south,
> Lands bathed in sweeter, rarer, healthier air, valleys and mountain cliffs,
> The fields of Nature long prepared and fallow, the silent, cyclic chemistry,
> The slow and steady ages plodding, the unoccupied surface ripening, the rich ores forming beneath;
> At last the New arriving, assuming, taking possession,
> A swarming and busy race settling and organizing everywhere,
> Ships coming in from the whole round world, and going out to the whole world,
> To India and China and Australia and the thousand island paradises of the Pacific,
> Populous cities, the latest inventions, the steamers on the rivers, the railroads with many a thrifty
>   farm, with machinery,
> And wood and wheat and the grape, and diggings of yellow gold.[36]

Whitman's image of the California dream was the mythic sequel to Bishop Berkeley's verses on America.

By 1890 the Indians had gone from the range to the reservation, the nation had been traversed by a grid of railroads, and the Superintendent of the Census had declared:

> At present the unsettled area has been so broken into by isolated bodies of settlement that there can hardly be said to be a frontier line. In the discussion of its extent, its westward movement, etc., it can not, therefore, any longer have a place in the census reports.[37]

In the same year, 1890, James G. Blaine, a former Secretary of State and presidential nominee of 1884, said, "Our great demand is expansion. I mean expansion of trade with countries where we can find profitable exchanges. We are not seeking annexation of territory."[38] However, the necessity of annexing foreign land became indispensible to the new expansionism.[39] In the following decade the United States acquired the Philippine Islands, Hawaii and Puerto Rico and gained control of Cuba and, in 1903, the Panama Canal. The "frontier" simply shifted to international waters and foreign shores.

About 1890 the myth of the frontier waned in importance for most artists, although illustrations of clashes between Government troops and Indians continued to find a market in the popular magazines—and still provide thematic material for the motion pictures today. But during the years from 1825 to about 1880 paintings of the frontier and the West defined the national identity. Recent research has shown that the frontier was a harsh reality for most Americans because of crop failures, economic reversals, the traditional but enduring social stratification of the classes, and other vicissitudes. But the myth of the frontier—the renderings of heroic feats and the synthetic reconstructions of grand landscape vistas—was what most appealed to a young nation bent on conquering and cultivating a continent.

With opinions typical of their time and taking their cues from literary antecedents, artists were engaged in making art out of the material at hand. However, the artists had a reciprocal relationship to contemporary social, political and cultural developments; their paintings, widely exhibited and reproduced, in part contributed to the consolidation of national attitudes and the implementation of national policy. The concept of the Indian as savage, "primitive," and outside the society of the white man, sanctioned the inhumane treatment of the Indians and their removal to reservation camps. The visualization of the American pioneer as the super-hero encouraged western migration, justified geographical expansion, and fostered ideas about "rugged individualism."

The art tells us the stories we wanted to hear. But by probing their deeper meanings, we can learn more about ourselves and the development of our consciousness throughout the nineteenth century.

Notes

1. *The Works of George Berkeley, D. D.*, ed. Alexander C. Fraser (4 vols.; Oxford, 1901), IV, pp. 364-65.

2. Ralph Waldo Emerson, "The Poet," *The Works of Ralph Waldo Emerson*, ed. J. E. Cabot (10 vols.; Boston and New York, 1883), III, p. 41.

3. The birth and death dates of the artists discussed are noted in the Catalogue of the Exhibition. Brief biographies of many "frontier" artists may be found in Perry T. Rathbone, *Westward the Way* (St. Louis: City Art Museum, 1954) and Larry Curry, *The American West* (New York: The Viking Press, Inc. in association with the Los Angeles County Museum of Art, 1972).

4. Quoted in John W. McCoubrey, *American Art: 1700-1960, Sources and Documents* (Englewood Cliffs, New Jersey: Prentice-Hall, Inc., 1965), p. 102.

5. Quoted in James Thomas Flexner, *That Wilder Image* (New York: Bonanza Books, 1962), p. ix.

6. Asher B. Durand, "Letters on Landscape Painting. Letter II," *Crayon*, I (January 17, 1855), pp. 34-35. Also quoted in Roger B. Stein *John Ruskin and Aesthetic Thought in America, 1840-1900* (Cambridge, Massachusetts: Harvard University Press, 1967), p. 14.

7. See Flexner, *op. cit.*, p. 78.

8. As early as 1824 William Cullin Bryant wrote "An Indian at the Burial-place of His Fathers" which went in part:

> They waste us—ay—like April snow
> In the warm noon, we shrink away;
> And fast they follow, as we go
> Toward the setting day—
> Till they shall fill the land, and we
> Are driven into the Western sea.

9. (1809-1893). His original watercolors were not available for the present exhibition.

10. William Brandon, *The American Heritage Book of Indians* (New York: American Heritage Publishing Co., Inc., 1961), p. 220.

11. See Lewis A. Shepard, *Cowboys, Indians, Trappers and Traders: Exhibition* (Amherst, Massachusetts: Amherst College, 1973), p. [8].

12. Frederic Jackson Turner, "The Significance of the Frontier in American History," *Frontier and Section: Selected Essays of Frederic Jackson Turner*, intro. by Ray Allen Billington (Englewood Cliffs, N.J.: Prentice-Hall, Inc., 1961), p. 38.

13. Henry Nash Smith in *Virgin Land: The American West as Symbol and Myth* (Cambridge, Massachusetts: Harvard University Press, reissued with a new preface, 1970), pp. 133-144, has pointed out that the agrarian ideal of frontier egalitarianism never occurred.

14. These two popular history paintings were exhibited in New York in the early 1850s; an engraving after *Boone's First View of Kentucky* was published in the American Art-Union's widely circulated *Bulletin* in May 1850. See Francis S. Grubar, *William Ranney: Painter of the Early West* (Washington, D. C.: The Corcoran Gallery of Art, 1962), pp. 32-33, 40-41.

15. This work was engraved by the French firm, Goupil and Company. See E. Maurice Bloch, *George Caleb Bingham: The Evolution of an Artist* (2 vols.; Berkeley and Los Angeles: University of California Press, 1967), I, pp. 120-23.

16. Turner, *op. cit.*, p. 44.

17. See Smith, *op. cit.*, particularly the chapter, "Leatherstocking and the Problem of Social Order," pp. 59-70.

18. Robert F. Westervelt, "The Whig Painter of Missouri," *The American Art Journal*, II:1 (Spring, 1970), 46.

19. Quoted in Museum of Fine Arts, Boston, *American Paintings in the Museum of Fine Arts, Boston* (2 vol.; Boston: Museum of Fine Arts, 1969), I, 30.

20. Brandon, *op. cit.*, pp. 242-44, has pointed out that one of the major differences between European and Indian culture was rooted in the matter of property; the European simply could not comprehend a view of life in which acquisition of property was not paramount.

21. Quoted in McCoubrey, *op. cit.*, p. 100.

22. See Roy Harvey Pearce, *The Savages of America: A Study of the Indian and the Idea of Civilization* (2d ed. rev.; Baltimore: The Johns Hopkins Press, 1965).

23. Quoted in Smith, *op. cit.*, p. 37.

24. The democratically intended legislation was rarely egalitarian in practice. However, the Homestead Act was important to the anti-slavery North; small farms could not sustain crews of slaves. See Smith, *op. cit.*, pp. 165-73.

25. According to Grubar, *op. cit.*, p. 41, the main figure may be Jim Bridger, called the "Daniel Boone of the Rocky Mountains."

26. Quoted in Matthew Josephson, *The Robber Barons: The Great American Capitalists, 1861-1901* (New York: Harcourt, Brace & World, Inc., 1962, first published in 1934).

27. *Ibid.*

28. During the 1870s the publishing firm Currier and Ives issued a number of lithographs of trains, the most notable of which was titled *Across the Continent: Westward the Course of Empire Takes its Way.*

29. "The Autobiography of Worthington Whittredge, 1820-1910," ed. John I. H. Baur, *Brooklyn Museum Journal*, II (1942), 64.

30. Moran told the art critic G. W. Sheldon: "...While I desired to tell truly of Nature, I did not wish to realize the scene literally, but to preserve and to convey its true impression." Quoted in G. W. Sheldon, *American Painters* (New York, 1881), pp. 125-26, and requoted in William H. Truettner and Robin Bolton-Smith, *National Parks and the American Landscape* (Washington, D. C.: Smithsonian Institution Press, 1972), p. 23.

31. S. G. W. Benjamin, "A Pioneer of the Palette: Thomas Moran," *Magazine of Art*, V (February, 1882), 92.

32. *Ibid.*

33. Kevin Starr, *Americans and the California Dream, 1850-1915* (New York: Oxford University Press, 1973), p. 79.

34. Charles Christian Nahl (1818-1878) was one of the most interesting artists working in this genre. His *Sunday Morning at the Mines*, Collection E. B. Crocker Art Gallery, Sacramento, is a compendium of miners' activities: fighting, reading, washing clothes, writing letters, playing cards, cheating, and racing horses.

35. The painting, Collection E. B. Crocker Art Gallery, was not available for the exhibition.

36. Quoted in Starr, *op. cit.*, p. 417.

37. Quoted in Turner, *op. cit.*, p. 37.

38. Quoted in Norman A. Graebner, Gilbert C. Fite, and Philip L. White, *A History of the American People* (New York: McGraw-Hill Book Company, 1970), pp. 837-38.

39. *Ibid.*

Fig. 1. THOMAS COLE. *American Lake Scene,* 1844. Oil on canvas, 18 1/4 x 24 1/2. The Detroit Institute of Arts, Gift of Douglas F. Roby

Fig. 2. ASHER B. DURAND. *The American Wilderness*, 1864. Oil on canvas,
25 1/4 x 40. Cincinnati Art Museum, The Edwin and Virginia Irwin Memorial

Fig. 3. JOSHUA SHAW. *On the Susquehanna*, 1839. Oil on canvas, 39 x 55 1/2. Museum of
Fine Arts, Boston, M. and M. Karolik Collection

Fig. 4. SANFORD ROBINSON GIFFORD. *In the Wilderness*, 1860. Oil on canvas, 30 x 54. The Toledo Museum of Art, Gift of Florence Scott Libbey 1951

Fig. 5. TITIAN RAMSAY PEALE. *Canis Lupus*, (1819-20). Watercolor, 5 1/2 x 8. James H. Maroney, New York

Fig. 6. GEORGE CATLIN. *Prairie Bluffs Burning*, 1832. Oil on canvas, 11 1/8 x 14 3/8. National Collection of Fine Arts, Smithsonian Institution, Washington, D. C., Gift of Mrs. Sarah Harrison

Fig. 7. GEORGE CATLIN. *Sioux Indians on Snowshoes Lancing Buffalo*. Oil on canvas mounted on masonite, 19 1/2 x 27 5/8. National Collection of Fine Arts, Smithsonian Institution, Washington, D. C., Gift of Mrs. Sarah Harrison

Fig. 8. GEORGE CATLIN. *Buffalo Chase—Bull Protecting Cow and Calf*, 1830s. Oil on canvas mounted on aluminum, 22 5/8 x 27 5/8. National Collection of Fine Arts, Smithsonian Institution, Washington, D. C., Gift of Mrs. Sarah Harrison

Fig. 9. ALFRED JACOB MILLER. *Beating a Retreat*, circa 1842. Oil on canvas, 29 x 36. Museum of Fine Arts, Boston,
M. and M. Karolik Collection

Fig. 10. JOHN MIX STANLEY. *A Halt on the Prairie for a Smoke*. Oil on canvas, 8 7/8 x 11 1/4. The Detroit Institute of Arts, Gift of Mrs. William Fitzhugh Edwards

Fig. 11. SETH EASTMAN. *Lacrosse Playing Among the Sioux Indians*, 1851. Oil on canvas, 28 3/16 x 40 3/4. Corcoran Gallery of Art, Washington, D. C., Gift of William Wilson Corcoran

Fig. 12. HENRY F. FARNY. *The Last Vigil*, 1881. Oil on canvas, 49 x 39 1/2. Mrs. George A. Rentschler, New York

Fig. 13. THOMAS COLE. *Scene from "The Last of the Mohicans,"* 1827. Oil on canvas, 25 5/16 x 34 15/16. Wadsworth Atheneum, Hartford, Bequest of Alfred Smith, 1868

Fig. 14. CHARLES DEAS. *The Voyageurs*, 1846. Oil on canvas, 13 x 20 1/2. Museum of Fine Arts, Boston, M. and M. Karolik Collection

Fig. 15. ALVAN T. FISHER. *Trappers Discover the Smoke of an Indian Camp*, circa 1842. Oil on canvas, 22 x 27. Amherst College Collection, Massachusetts, Gift of Herbert W. Plimpton, in honor of his father, Hollis W. Plimpton '15. Photograph courtesy of Kennedy Galleries, Inc., New York

Fig. 16. Arthur F. Tait. *American Frontier Life*, 1852. Oil on canvas, 24 3/8 x 26 1/4. Yale University Art Gallery, New Haven, Whitney Collection of Sporting Art, given in memory of Harry Payne Whitney (B.A. 1894) and Payne Whitney (B.A. 1898) by Francis P. Garvan (B.A. 1897)

Fig. 17. WILLIAM RANNEY. *Daniel Boone's First View of Kentucky*, 1849. Oil on canvas, 37 1/2 x 54. National Cowboy Hall of Fame and Western Heritage Center, Oklahoma City

Fig. 18. WILLIAM RANNEY. *Squire Boone Crossing the Mountain with Stores for His Brother Daniel, Encamped in the Wilds of Kentucky*, 1852. Oil on canvas, 36 x 32 1/2. Miss Amelia Peabody, Boston

Fig. 19. GEORGE CALEB BINGHAM. *Daniel Boone Escorting Settlers Through the Cumberland Gap*, 1851-52. Oil on canvas, 36 x 52. Washington University Gallery of Art, St. Louis

Fig. 20. GEORGE CALEB BINGHAM. *The Squatters*, 1850. Oil on canvas, 25 x 30. Museum of Fine Arts, Boston

Fig. 21. THOMAS COLE. *Home in the Woods*, 1847. Oil on canvas, 44 x 66. Reynolda House, Inc., Winston-Salem, North Carolina

Fig. 22. FREDERIC EDWIN CHURCH. *Scene in the Catskill Mountains*, 1852. Oil on canvas, 32 x 48. Walker Art Center, Minneapolis

Fig. 23. SANFORD ROBINSON GIFFORD. *Twilight on Hunter Mountain*, 1866. Oil on canvas, 30 1/2 x 54. Vose Galleries of Boston

Fig. 24. JOHN MIX STANLEY. *A Buffalo Hunt on the Southwestern Prairie*. Oil on canvas, 40 1/2 x 60 5/8. National Collection of Fine Arts, Smithsonian Institution, Washington, D. C., Gift of the Misses Henry (daughters of a former Secretary of the Smithsonian Institution)

Fig. 25. CHARLES FERDINAND WIMAR. *Buffalo Hunt*, 1860. Oil on canvas, 36 x 60. Washington University Gallery of Art, St. Louis

Fig. 26. WILLIAM RANNEY. *Hunting Wild Horses*, 1846. Oil on canvas, 36 x 54 1/2. Joslyn Art Museum, Omaha, Northern Natural Gas Company Collection

Fig. 27. CHARLES DEAS. *The Prairie Fire*, 1847. Oil on canvas, 29 x 35 7/8. The Brooklyn Museum, Gift of Mr. and Mrs. A. B. Martin

Fig. 28. JOHANNES ADAM SIMON OERTEL. *The War Path*, 1855. Oil on canvas, 30 x 24 3/4. Hirschl and Adler Galleries, New York

Below Fig. 29. CHARLES FERDINAND WIMAR. *The Attack on an Emigrant Train*, 1856. Oil on canvas, 55 1/4 x 79. The University of Michigan Museum of Art, Ann Arbor, Bequest of Henry C. Lewis

Fig. 30. JULES TAVERNIER. *Attack by Indians near Chimney Rock*. Oil on canvas, 28 3/4 x 48 3/4. Bohemian Club, San Francisco

Fig. 31. GEORGE DOUGLAS BREWERTON. *Mojave Desert.* Oil on canvas, 30 x 44. The Oakland Museum

Fig. 32. THOMAS PRITCHARD ROSSITER. *Opening of the Wilderness*, circa 1846-50. Oil on canvas, 17 3/4 x 32 1/2. Museum of Fine Arts, Boston, M. and M. Karolik Collection

Fig. 33. THOMAS P. OTTER. *On the Road*, 1860. Oil on canvas, 22 1/2 x 45 3/4. William Rockhill Nelson Gallery of Art and Atkins Museum of Fine Arts, Kansas City, Nelson Fund

Fig. 34. THEODOR KAUFMANN. *Railway Train Attacked by Indians*, 1867. Oil on canvas, 36 1/4 x 56 1/4. H. Richard Dietrich, Jr., Philadelphia

Fig. 35. WILLIAM RANNEY. *Advice on the Prairie*, 1853. Oil on canvas, 40 x 54. Mr. and Mrs. J. Maxwell Moran, Paoli, Pennsylvania

Fig. 36. BENJAMIN FRANKLIN RINEHART. *The Emigrant Train Bedding Down for the Night*, 1867. Oil on canvas, 40 x 70. Corcoran Gallery of Art, Washington, D. C., Gift of Mr. and Mrs. Lansdell K. Christie

Fig. 37. SAMUEL COLMAN. *Ships of the Plains*, 1872. Oil on canvas, 48 x 96 1/4. The Union League Club, New York. Photograph courtesy of Frick Art Reference Library, New York

Fig. 38. Albert Bierstadt. *Platte River, Nebraska,* 1863. Oil on canvas, 36 x 57 1/2. Jones Library, Amherst, Massachusetts

Fig. 39. THOMAS WORTHINGTON WHITTREDGE. *Crossing the Ford, Platte River, Colorado*, 1868-70. Oil on canvas, 40 x 68. The Century Association, New York. Photograph courtesy of Frick Art Reference Library, New York

Fig. 40. SAMUEL COLMAN. *Emigrant Train, Colorado*, 1872. Oil on canvas, 19 1/2 x 40. St. Johnsbury Athenaeum, Vermont

Fig. 41. THOMAS WORTHINGTON WHITTREDGE. *On the Plains, Colorado,* 1877. Oil on canvas, 30 x 50. St. Johnsbury Athenaeum, Vermont

Fig. 42. THOMAS MORAN. *The Mirage,* 1879. Oil on canvas, 24 3/8 x 61 5/16. Kimbell Art Museum, Fort Worth

Fig. 43. WILLIAM SIDNEY MOUNT. *California News*, 1850. Oil on canvas, 21 1/8 x 20 1/4. Suffolk Museum and Carriage House, Stony Brook, Long Island, Melville Collection

Below Fig. 44. JOSEPH HARRINGTON. *Discovery of the Comstock Lode*, 1875. Oil on canvas, 43 x 60 1/4. The Fine Arts Museums of San Francisco

Fig. 45. MARTIN. *The Forty-Niners*, circa 1850. Oil on canvas, 39 1/2 x 72. Hirschl and
Adler Galleries, New York

Fig. 46. RUFUS WRIGHT. *The Card Players*, 1882. Oil on canvas, 24 1/4
x 29 1/2. The Oakland Museum, Gift of the Kahn Foundation

Fig. 47. ERNEST NARJOT. *Gold Rush Camp*, 1882. Oil on canvas, 40 x 55 1/2. The Los Angeles Athletic Club

Fig. 48. ALBERTUS D. O. BROWERE. *South of Tuolumne City*, 1861. Oil on canvas, 30 x 44. The Oakland Museum, Gift of the Kahn Foundation

Fig. 49. EDWIN DEAKIN. *Mount Tallac*, 1877. Oil on canvas, 30 x 50 1/4. The California Historical Society, San Francisco

Fig. 50. WILLIAM KEITH. *California Pines*, 1878. Oil on canvas, 36 1/4 x 72 1/2. Los Angeles County Museum of Art, Gift of Museum Patrons Association

Fig. 51. THOMAS HILL. *Yosemite Valley*. Oil on canvas, 53 1/2 x 35. The Oakland Museum, Gift of Mr. Fred Maxwell

Fig. 52. WILLIAM HAHN. *Return from the Hunt, Sierras*, 1880. Oil on canvas, 36 x 20. The Los Angeles Athletic Club

Fig. 53. WILLIAM HAHN. *Return from the Bear Hunt*, 1882. Oil on canvas, 55 x 89. The Oakland Museum

Fig. 54. OTTO SOMMER. *Westward Ho!*, 1867-68. Oil on canvas, 44 x 74 1/2. The Los Angeles Athletic Club

Fig. 55. WILLIAM HAHN. *Mexican Cattle Drivers*, 1883. Oil on canvas, 34 1/2 x 60. J. N. Bartfield Art Galleries Inc., New York

Fig. 56. JAMES WALKER. *Vaqueros at the Roundup*, 1877. Oil on canvas, 30 3/8 x 50 3/8. Carl Schaefer Dentzel, Los Angeles

Fig. 57. JAMES WALKER. *Californios at the Horse Roundup.* Oil on canvas, 30 1/2 x 50 1/2. Carl Schaefer Dentzel, Los Angeles

Fig. 58. WILLIAM HAHN. *Market Scene, Sansome Street, San Francisco*. Oil on canvas, 60 x 96. E. B. Crocker Art Gallery, Sacramento (Not included in the exhibition.)

Lenders to the Exhibition

Amherst College, Massachusetts; J. N. Bartfield Art Galleries Inc., New York; The Beinecke Rare Book and Manuscript Library, Yale University, New Haven; Bohemian Club, San Francisco; The Brooklyn Museum; The California Historical Society, San Francisco; The Century Association, New York; Cincinnati Art Museum; Corcoran Gallery of Art, Washington, D. C.; The Detroit Institute of Arts; M. H. De Young Memorial Museum, San Francisco; Hirschl and Adler Galleries, New York; Indiana University, Bloomington; Jones Library, Amherst, Massachusetts; Joslyn Art Museum, Omaha, Northern Natural Gas Company Collection; Kimbell Art Museum, Fort Worth; The Los Angeles Athletic Club; Los Angeles County Museum of Art; Museum of Fine Arts, Boston; National Collection of Fine Arts, Smithsonian Institution, Washington, D. C.; National Cowboy Hall of Fame and Western Heritage Center, Oklahoma City; William Rockhill Nelson Gallery of Art and Atkins Museum of Fine Arts, Kansas City; The Oakland Museum; Peabody Museum of Archeology and Ethnology, Harvard University, Cambridge, Massachusetts; Pioneer Museum and Haggin Galleries, Stockton, California; Reynolda House, Winston-Salem, North Carolina; St. Johnsbury Athenaeum, Vermont; Suffolk Museum and Carriage House, Stony Brook, Long Island; The Toledo Museum of Art; The Union League Club, New York; The University of Michigan Museum of Art, Ann Arbor; Vose Galleries of Boston; Wadsworth Atheneum, Hartford; Walker Art Center, Minneapolis; Washington University Gallery of Art, St. Louis; Yale University Art Gallery, New Haven.

H. Richard Dietrich, Jr., Philadelphia; Carl Schaefer Dentzel, Los Angeles; Mr. and Mrs. Jack Frost, Santa Monica; James H. Maroney, New York; Mr. and Mrs. J. Maxwell Moran, Paoli, Pennsylvania; Miss Amelia Peabody, Boston; Mrs. George A. Rentschler, New York; Private Collection.

Catalogue of the Exhibition

Measurements are in inches, height preceding width.

ANONYMOUS

1. *Forest Burial*, circa 1860
   Oil on canvas, 23 3/4 x 32 1/4
   Ira Spanierman Gallery, New York

CASSILLY ADAMS (1843-1921)

2. *Playing Cards*
   Oil on canvas, 12 x 17 3/4
   Carl Schaefer Dentzel, Los Angeles

ALBERT BIERSTADT (1830-1902)

3. *Platte River, Nebraska*, 1863
   Oil on canvas, 36 x 57 1/2
   Jones Library, Amherst, Massachusetts

4. *The Trapper's Camp*, 1861
   Oil on mill-board, 13 x 19
   Yale University Art Gallery, New Haven, Whitney Collection of Sporting Art, given in memory of Harry Payne Whitney (B.A. 1894) and Payne Whitney (B.A. 1898) by Francis P. Garvan (B.A. 1897)

GEORGE CALEB BINGHAM (1811-1879)

5. *The Concealed Enemy*, 1845
   Oil on canvas, 28 1/2 x 35 1/2
   Peabody Museum of Archeology and Ethnology, Harvard University, Cambridge, Massachusetts

6. *Daniel Boone Escorting Settlers Through the Cumberland Gap*, 1851-52
   Oil on canvas, 36 x 52
   Washington University Gallery of Art, St. Louis

7. *The Squatters*, 1850
   Oil on canvas, 25 x 30
   Museum of Fine Arts, Boston

GEORGE DOUGLAS BREWERTON (1827-1901)

8. *Mojave Desert*
   Oil on canvas, 30 x 44
   The Oakland Museum

ALBERTUS D. O. BROWERE (1814-1889)

9. *South of Tuolumne City*, 1861
   Oil on canvas, 30 x 44
   The Oakland Museum, Gift of the Kahn Foundation

EUGEN CAMERE (active 1860s)

10. *Mike Shuler's Freighting Outfit*
    Oil on canvas, 18 3/4 x 24 1/4
    Pioneer Museum and Haggin Galleries, Stockton, California, Gift of Mrs. Louise B. Reuter

WILLIAM DE LA MONTAIGNE CARY (1840-1922)

11. *James Bridger and Sir William Drummond Stewart*, 1867-72
    Oil on canvas, 14 1/4 x 18
    Carl Schaefer Dentzel, Los Angeles

GEORGE CATLIN (1796-1872)

12. *Buffalo Chase—Bull Protecting Cow and Calf*, 1830s
Oil on canvas mounted on aluminum, 22 5/8 x 27 5/8
National Collection of Fine Arts, Smithsonian Institution, Washington, D. C., Gift of Mrs. Sarah Harrison

13. *Prairie Bluffs Burning*, 1832
Oil on canvas, 11 1/8 x 14 3/8
National Collection of Fine Arts, Smithsonian Institution, Washington, D. C., Gift of Mrs. Sarah Harrison

14. *Sioux Indians on Snowshoes Lancing Buffalo*
Oil on canvas mounted on masonite, 19 1/2 x 27 5/8
National Collection of Fine Arts, Smithsonian Institution, Washington, D. C., Gift of Mrs. Sarah Harrison

FREDERIC EDWIN CHURCH (1826-1900)

15. *Scene in the Catskill Mountains*, 1852
Oil on canvas, 32 x 48
Walker Art Center, Minneapolis

THOMAS COLE (1801-1849)

16. *American Lake Scene*, 1844
Oil on canvas, 18 1/4 x 24 1/2
The Detroit Institute of Arts. Gift of Douglas F. Roby

17. *Home in the Woods*, 1847
Oil on canvas, 44 x 66
Reynolda House, Inc., Winston-Salem, North Carolina

18. *Scene from "The Last of the Mohicans,"* 1827
Oil on canvas, 25 5/16 x 34 15/16
Wadsworth Atheneum, Hartford, Bequest of Alfred Smith, 1868

SAMUEL COLMAN (1832-1920)

19. *Emigrant Train, Colorado*, 1872
Oil on canvas, 19 1/2 x 40
St. Johnsbury Athenaeum, Vermont

20. *Ships of the Plains*, 1872
Oil on canvas, 48 x 96 1/4
The Union League Club, New York

EDWIN DEAKIN (1838-1923)

21. *Mount Tallac*, 1877
Oil on canvas, 30 x 50 1/4
The California Historical Society, San Francisco

CHARLES DEAS (1818-1867)

22. *The Prairie Fire*, 1847
Oil on canvas, 29 x 35 7/8
The Brooklyn Museum, Gift of Mr. and Mrs. A. B. Martin

23. *The Voyageurs*, 1846
Oil on canvas, 13 x 20 1/2
Museum of Fine Arts, Boston, M. and M. Karolik Collection

ASHER B. DURAND (1796-1886)

24. *The American Wilderness*, 1864
Oil on canvas, 24 1/4 x 40
Cincinnati Art Museum, The Edwin and Virginia Irwin Memorial

SETH EASTMAN (1808-1875)

25. *Indian on the Lookout, circa* 1841-48
Oil on canvas, 22 x 29 3/4
Joslyn Art Museum, Omaha, Northern Natural Gas Company Collection

26. *Lacrosse Playing Among the Sioux Indians*, 1851
Oil on canvas, 28 3/16 x 40 3/4
Corcoran Gallery of Art, Washington, D. C., Gift of William Wilson Corcoran

HENRY F. FARNY (1847-1916)

27. *The Last Vigil*, 1881
Oil on canvas, 49 x 39 1/2
Mrs. George A. Rentschler, New York

28. *Toilers of the Plains*, 1882
Oil on canvas, 22 1/4 x 40
Cincinnati Art Museum, The Edward Foote Hinkle Collection

ALVAN T. FISHER (1792-1863)

29. *Trappers Discover the Smoke of an Indian Camp, circa* 1842
Oil on canvas, 22 x 27
Amherst College Collection, Massachusetts, Gift of Herbert W. Plimpton, in honor of his father, Hollis W. Plimpton '15

SANFORD ROBINSON GIFFORD (1823-1880)

30. *In the Wilderness*, 1860
Oil on canvas, 30 x 54
The Toledo Museum of Art, Gift of Florence Scott Libbey 1951

31. *Twilight on Hunter Mountain*, 1866
Oil on canvas, 30 1/2 x 54
Vose Galleries of Boston

WILLIAM HAHN (1829-1887)

32. *Mexican Cattle Drivers*, 1883
Oil on canvas, 34 1/2 x 60
J. N. Bartfield Art Galleries, Inc., New York

33. *Return from the Bear Hunt*, 1882
Oil on canvas, 55 x 89
The Oakland Museum

34. *Return from the Hunt, Sierras*, 1880
Oil on canvas, 36 x 20
The Los Angeles Athletic Club

JOSEPH HARRINGTON (1841-1900)

35. *Discovery of the Comstock Lode*, 1875
Oil on canvas, 43 x 60 1/4
The Fine Arts Museums of San Francisco

JAMES McDOUGAL HART (1828-1901)

36. *The Adirondacks*
Oil on canvas, 41 x 67 1/2
J. N. Bartfield Art Galleries Inc., New York

THOMAS HILL (1829-1908)

37. *Yosemite Valley*
Oil on canvas, 53 1/2 x 35
The Oakland Museum, Gift of Mr. Fred Maxwell

THEODOR KAUFMANN (1814-after 1887)

38. *Railway Train Attacked by Indians*, 1867
Oil on canvas, 36 1/4 x 56 1/4
H. Richard Dietrich, Jr., Philadelphia

WILLIAM KEITH (1838-1911)

39. *California Pines*, 1878
Oil on canvas, 36 1/4 x 72 1/2
Los Angeles County Museum of Art, Gift of Museum Patrons Association

EMANUEL LEUTZE (1816-1868)

40. *Westward the Course of Empire Takes Its Way*, 1861
Oil on canvas 33 3/8 x 43 3/8
National Collection of Fine Arts, Smithsonian Institution, Washington, D. C., Bequest of Miss Sara Carr Upton

MARTIN (active 1850s)

41. *The Forty-Niners*, circa 1850
Oil on canvas, 39 1/2 x 72
Hirschl and Adler Galleries, New York

ALFRED JACOB MILLER (1810-1874)

42. *Beating a Retreat*, circa 1842
Oil on canvas, 29 x 36
Museum of Fine Arts, Boston, M. and M. Karolik Collection

43. *The Lost Greenhorn*
Oil on canvas, 15 1/4 x 23
Carl Schaefer Dentzel, Los Angeles

THOMAS MORAN (1837-1925)

44. *The Mirage*, 1879
Oil on canvas, 24 3/8 x 61 5/16
Kimbell Art Museum, Fort Worth

WILLIAM SIDNEY MOUNT (1807-1868)

45. *California News*, 1850
Oil on canvas, 21 1/8 x 20 1/4
Suffolk Museum and Carriage House, Stony Brook, Long Island, Melville Collection

ERNEST NARJOT (1826-1898)

46. *Danger Ahead for the Wagon Train*
Oil on canvas, 33 x 52 1/2
Carl Schaefer Dentzel, Los Angeles

47. *Gold Rush Camp*, 1882
Oil on canvas, 40 x 55 1/2
The Los Angeles Athletic Club

JOHANNES ADAM SIMON OERTEL (1823-1909)

48. *The War Path*, 1855
Oil on canvas, 30 x 24 3/4
Hirschl and Adler Galleries, New York

THOMAS P. OTTER (active 1855-1867)

49. *On the Road*, 1860
Oil on canvas, 22 1/2 x 45 3/4
William Rockhill Nelson Gallery of Art and Atkins Museum of Fine Arts, Kansas City, Nelson Fund

WILLIAM SAMUEL PARROTT (1844-1915)

50. *Shoshone Falls, Snake River, Idaho*
Oil on canvas, 42 x 60
The Fine Arts Museums of San Francisco

TITIAN RAMSAY PEALE (1800-1885)

51. *Canis Lupus* (1819-20)
Watercolor, 5 1/2 x 8
James H. Maroney, New York

52. *Sioux Lodge*, 1819
Watercolor, 6 1/4 x 9
Private Collection

WILLIAM RANNEY (1813-1857)

53. *Advice on the Prairie*, 1853
Oil on canvas, 40 x 54
Mr. and Mrs. J. Maxwell Moran, Paoli, Pennsylvania

54. *Daniel Boone's First View of Kentucky*, 1849
Oil on canvas, 37 1/2 x 54
National Cowboy Hall of Fame and Western Heritage Center, Oklahoma City

55. *Hunting Wild Horses*, 1846
Oil on canvas, 36 x 54 1/2
Joslyn Art Museum, Omaha, Northern Natural Gas Company Collection

56. *Prairie Burial*, 1848
Oil on canvas, 28 1/2 x 41
Mr. and Mrs. J. Maxwell Moran, Paoli, Pennsylvania

57. *Squire Boone Crossing the Mountain with Stores for His Brother Daniel, Encamped in the Wilds of Kentucky*, 1852
Oil on canvas, 36 x 32 1/2
Miss Amelia Peabody, Boston

BENJAMIN FRANKLIN RINEHART (1829-1885)

58. *The Emigrant Train Bedding Down for the Night*, 1867
Oil on canvas, 40 x 70
Corcoran Gallery of Art, Washington, D. C., Gift of Mr. and Mrs. Lansdell K. Christie

THOMAS PRITCHARD ROSSITER (1818-1871)

59. *Opening of the Wilderness*, circa 1846-50
Oil on canvas, 17 3/4 x 32 1/2
Museum of Fine Arts, Boston, M. and M. Karolik Collection

SAMUEL SEYMOUR (1797-1882)

60. *Kiowa Encampment*, 1820
Watercolor, 5 3/4 x 8
The Beinecke Rare Book and Manuscript Library, Yale University, New Haven

61. *Pawnee Council*, 1820
Watercolor, 5 7/8 x 8
The Beinecke Rare Book and Manuscript Library, Yale University, New Haven

JOSHUA SHAW (1776-1860)

62. *Coming of the White Man*, 1850
Oil on canvas, 25 x 36
Carl Schaefer Dentzel, Los Angeles

63. *Indians Hunting*
Oil on canvas, 21 x 30
Carl Schaefer Dentzel, Los Angeles

64. *On the Susquehanna*, 1839
Oil on canvas, 39 x 55 1/2
Museum of Fine Arts, Boston, M. and M. Karolik Collection

OTTO SOMMER (active 1860s)

65. *Westward Ho!*, 1867-68
Oil on canvas, 44 x 74 1/2
The Los Angeles Athletic Club

JOHN MIX STANLEY (1814-1872)

66. *Assiniboin Encampment on the Upper Missouri*
Oil on canvas, 7 7/8 x 10 7/8
The Detroit Institute of Arts, Gift of Mrs. William Fitzhugh Edwards

67. *A Buffalo Hunt on the Southwestern Prairie*
Oil on canvas, 40 1/2 x 60 5/8
National Collection of Fine Arts, Smithsonian Institution, Washington, D. C., Gift of the Misses Henry (daughters of a former Secretary of the Smithsonian Institution)

68. *A Halt on the Prairie for a Smoke*
Oil on canvas, 8 7/8 x 11 1/4
The Detroit Institute of Arts, Gift of Mrs. William Fitzhugh Edwards

ARTHUR F. TAIT (1819-1905)

69. *American Frontier Life*, 1852
Oil on canvas, 24 3/8 x 26 1/4
Yale University Art Gallery, New Haven, Whitney Collection of Sporting Art, given in memory of Harry Payne Whitney (B.A. 1894) and Payne Whitney (B.A. 1898) by Francis P. Garvan (B.A. 1897)

JULES TAVERNIER (1844-1887)

70. *Attack by Indians near Chimney Rock*
Oil on canvas, 28 3/4 x 48 3/4
Bohemian Club, San Francisco

EDWARD VISCHER (1809-1879)

71. *Giant Sequoia*
    Oil on canvas, 44 x 26
    Carl Schaefer Dentzel, Los Angeles

JAMES WALKER (1818-1889)

72. *Californios at the Horse Roundup*
    Oil on canvas, 30 1/2 x 50 1/2
    Carl Schaefer Dentzel, Los Angeles

73. *Vaqueros at the Roundup, 1877*
    Oil on canvas, 30 3/8 x 50 3/8
    Carl Schaefer Dentzel, Los Angeles

JOHN WEBBER (1752-1793)

74. *Nootka Sound*, 1784
    Watercolor and ink, 22 1/2 x 18 1/4
    Carl Schaefer Dentzel, Los Angeles

THOMAS WORTHINGTON WHITTREDGE (1820-1910)

75. *Crossing the Ford, Platte River, Colorado*, 1868-70
    Oil on canvas, 40 x 68
    The Century Association, New York

76. *On the Plains, Colorado*, 1877
    Oil on canvas, 30 x 50
    St. Johnsbury Athenaeum, Vermont

CHARLES FERDINAND WIMAR (1828-1862)

77. *The Attack on an Emigrant Train*, 1856
    Oil on canvas, 55 1/4 x 79
    The University of Michigan Museum of Art, Ann
       Arbor, Bequest of Henry C. Lewis

78. *Buffalo Hunt*, 1860
    Oil on canvas, 36 x 60
    Washington University Gallery of Art, St. Louis

RUFUS WRIGHT (1832-after 1882)

79. *The Card Players*, 1882
    Oil on canvas, 24 1/4 x 29 1/2
    The Oakland Museum, Gift of the Kahn Founda-
       tion

Addendum

WILLIAM HAHN

California Immigrants, 1879
    Oil on canvas, 26 x 42
    Mr. and Mrs. Jack Frost, Santa Monica

Photographic Credits:

E. Irving Blomstrann; Helga Photo Studio, Inc., New York;
Frick Art Reference Library, New York; Stone and Stec-
cati, San Francisco; V. Kriz; O. E. Nelson, New York;
Herbert P. Vose, Wellesley Hills, Mass.; Brenwasser, New
York.